Y0-BKL-638

CRICKETY CRICKET!

The Best-Loved Poems of James S. Tippett

CRICKETY CRICKET!

Harper & Row, Publishers, Inc.
New York, Evanston, San Francisco, London

The Best-Loved Poems
of James S. Tippett

Pictures by Mary Chalmers

Introduction by Donald J. Bissett

Most of the poems in this book originally appeared in COUNTING THE DAYS, I GO A-TRAVELING, I KNOW SOME LITTLE ANIMALS, I LIVE IN A CITY, I SPEND THE SUMMER, and A WORLD TO KNOW, published by Harper & Row, Publishers, Inc.

"Ducks in the Rain," "The Icicle," "My Christmas Tree," "Snowman," "Tracks in the Snow," "Windy Weather," and "The Year Moves On" originally appeared in PICTURES AND STORIES.

CRICKETY CRICKET! The Best-Loved Poems of James S. Tippett
Text copyright © 1973 by Martha K. Tippett
Illustrations copyright © 1973 by Mary Chalmers
Introduction copyright © 1973 by Harper & Row, Publishers, Inc.

All rights reserved. No part of this book may be used or reproduced in any manner whatsoever without written permission except in the case of brief quotations embodied in critical articles and reviews. Printed in the United States of America. For information address Harper & Row, Publishers, Inc., 10 East 53rd Street, New York, N.Y. 10022. Published simultaneously in Canada by Fitzhenry & Whiteside Limited, Toronto.

Library of Congress Catalog Card Number: 73-5498
Trade Standard Book Number: 06-026118-8
Harpercrest Standard Book Number: 06-026119-6

FIRST EDITION

CONTENTS

Introduction ix

PART ONE
I like the city . . .

IN THE CITY   3
APARTMENT HOUSES   4
GROCERIES   6
FOURTH FLOOR!   7
SOMETIMES   8
"SH!"   10
WITH MY BUILDING SET   11
THE ROOF   12
BUILDING A SKYSCRAPER   14
PEOPLE   16
THE PARK   17
PARK PLAY   18

PART TWO
. . . I love to go traveling . . .

TRAVELING   21
UNDERGROUND RUMBLING   22
TAXICABS   23
TRUCKS   24
FERRY-BOATS   27
TRAINS   28
UP IN THE AIR   30

PART THREE
Old Dog lay in the summer sun . . .

BAGGAGE   33
MOUNTAIN VIEWS   34
FAMILIAR FRIENDS   36
OVERALLS   38
HOUSE FOR BLUEBIRDS   40
WADING   42
GREEN FROG   43
TURTLE   44
CRICKET   45
GRASSHOPPER   46
WOOLLY BEAR CATERPILLAR   47
RED HEN   48
SMALL RED ANTS   49

KITTEN   50
MOTHER'S BOUQUETS   51
COMPANY   52
SUNNING   53
MY LITTLE RABBIT   54
DUCKS IN THE RAIN   56

PART FOUR
. . . tracks in the snow.

WHICH?   59
AUTUMN WOODS   60
BIRDS AT TWILIGHT   61
WINDY WEATHER   63
PLAY AFTER RAIN   64
TRACKS IN THE SNOW   66
THE ICICLE   68
SNOWMAN   69
A CITY STREET AT CHRISTMAS   70
COUNTING THE DAYS   71
MATILDA JANE AND I   72
WRAPPING PRESENTS   73
MY CHRISTMAS TREE   74
THE YEAR MOVES ON   76

Alphabetical List of Titles   79
Biographical Notes   83

Introduction

When I was working regularly with children in kindergarten and the primary grades, and sometimes in preschool programs, I was introduced to the perils of choosing poetry for young children. Daily reading aloud to five- and six-year-olds gave me the chance to see their reactions. The children were polite, eager and receptive, but they did not like all the poems.

Some of the poems amused them temporarily. Some they tolerated because I loved them. They liked the rhythm in some, the language in others. Only occasionally did the children react in such a way that I became convinced a poem was getting through to them. I was disappointed.

There is a difference between a polite response and the complete absorption a young child has when a poem really gets inside him. I began to find poems here and there that stimulated the response I expected. I found also that certain poets—only a few—consistently wrote poems that were fascinating to young children. It was then I discovered James Tippett.

Tippett sees the world as the young child does. He looks with equal intensity at all things, and responds openly to what he sees. That is why his verses live on, although he began writing for children nearly fifty years ago.

I am pleased that so many of James Tippett's poems are again being made available to children in this collection. Children like Tippett's poems. They like the everyday experiences he writes about. His images are fresh and childlike. He has fun with words. Often he uses a very simple rhythmic pattern and predictable rhymes that give security to the youngest child and make the verses easy to follow and memorize. Most of all, he has that unusual ability to see and write about things that are important to young children.

It's easier to see and feel than to explain. Take this book to a child. The child will show you.

Donald J. Bissett
Detroit, Michigan
April 1973

PART ONE
I like the city . . .

IN THE CITY

I like the city;
I find many things to do.
I play in the park,
I go to the zoo.

In my apartment
I have toys and games
And so many picture books
I can't tell their names.

I stand at my windows,
I see a whole fleet
Of streetcars and taxis
And trucks in the street.

APARTMENT HOUSES

Apartment houses on our street
Stand side by side.
Some of them are narrow.
Some are wide.

Some of them are low,
Some are high;
Some of them have towers
That reach into the sky.

All of them have windows,
Oh, so many!
There is not one house
That doesn't have any.

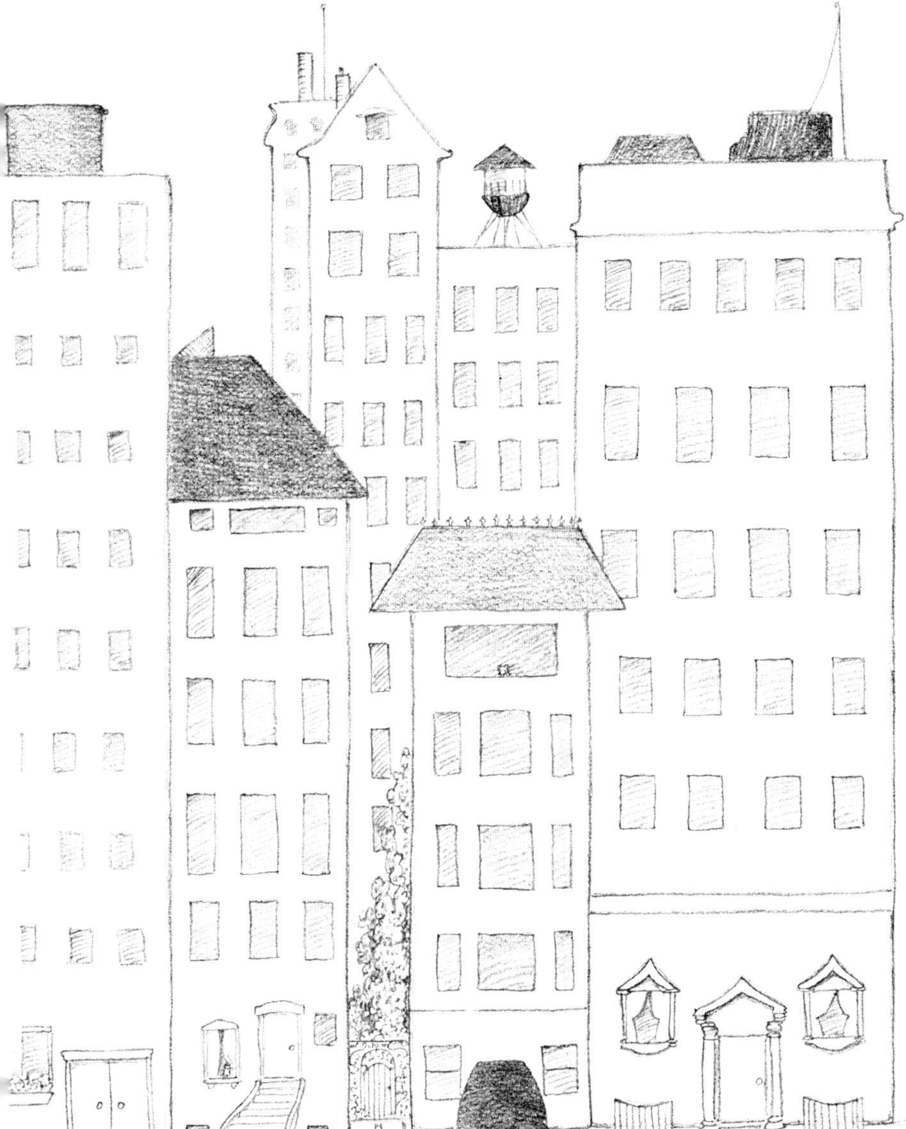

GROCERIES

The store around the corner
Has groceries to sell.
I go there with my mother;
I like that very well.

We look in the store windows
As we walk down the street.
We bring home many packages
Of groceries to eat.

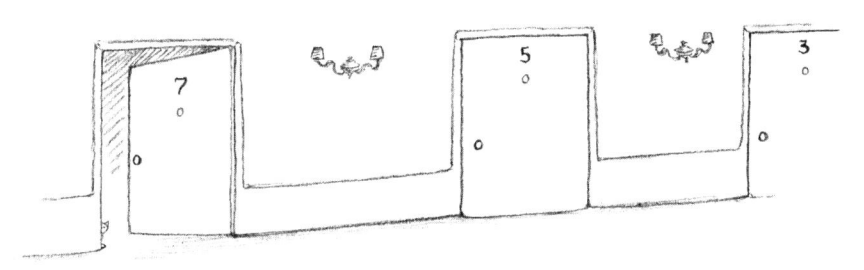

FOURTH FLOOR!

"Fourth floor!"
Is what I say
When I come in
From play.

My home
Is on that floor.
It has a "seven"
On the door.

Six other doors
Are on our hall
With a different family
Behind them all.

SOMETIMES

Sometimes
I sail my boat
In the bathtub.

Sometimes
I beat my drum
Rub-a-dub-dub.

Sometimes
I make a house
Of Mother's chairs.

Sometimes
I'm bears and tigers
In their lairs.

Sometimes
I like to bounce
My rubber ball.

Sometimes
I drive my horses
In the hall.

"SH!"

"Sh!" says Mother,
"Sh!" says Father.
"Running in the hall
Is a very great bother.

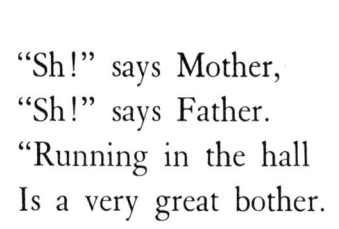

"Mrs. Grumpy Grundy,
Who lives down below,
Will come right up
First thing you know."

"Sh!" says Father,
"Sh!" says Mother.
"Can't you play a quiet game
Of some kind or other?"

WITH MY BUILDING SET

I can make bridges;
I can make trains;
I can make towers;
I can make cranes.

Here in our house
I can make them all
Solid and strong
So they will not fall.

I take steel pieces
And bolts and nuts;
I take my wrench
That opens and shuts.

My building set
Has everything in it.
I can make something
In less than a minute.

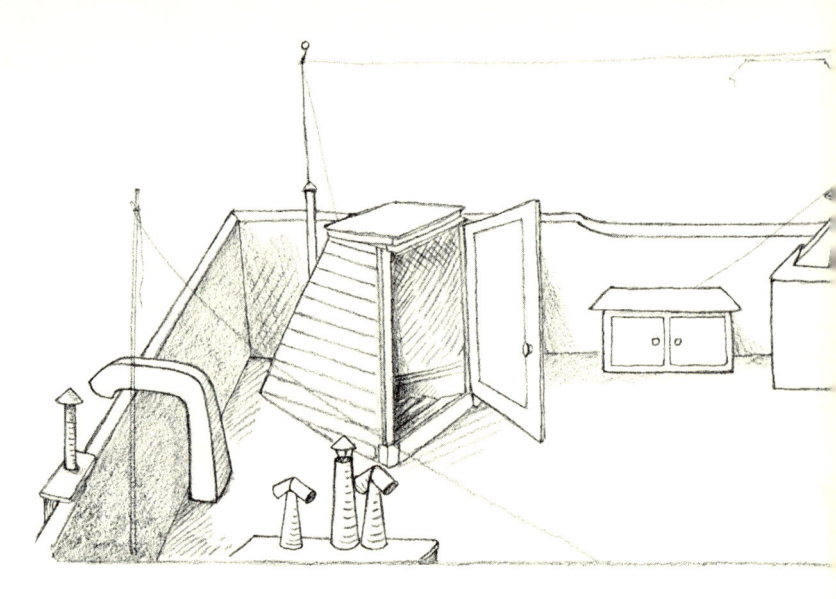

THE ROOF

At the top of the stairway
We open a door
And there is the roof
Spread out like a floor.

There are little roof-houses
Behind which we hide
And many tall pipes
And a wall at the side.

And stretched from poles
Are lines for clothes
And more radio wires
Than anyone knows.

Our roof is an interesting
Place to play.
I like to go there
Whenever I may.

BUILDING A SKYSCRAPER

They're building a skyscraper
Near our street.
Its height will be nearly
One thousand feet.

It covers completely
A city block.
They drilled its foundation
Through solid rock.

They made its framework
Of great steel beams
With riveted joints
And welded seams.

A swarm of workmen
Strain and strive
Like busy bees
In a honeyed hive

Building the skyscraper
Into the air
While crowds of people
Stand and stare.

Higher and higher
The tall towers rise
Like Jacob's ladder
Into the skies.

PEOPLE

I suppose a thousand people
Are walking on the streets.
Father says nobody knows
Anyone he meets.

But I see Jack and Eugene
And John and Emily
Over in the park
Waving at me.

THE PARK

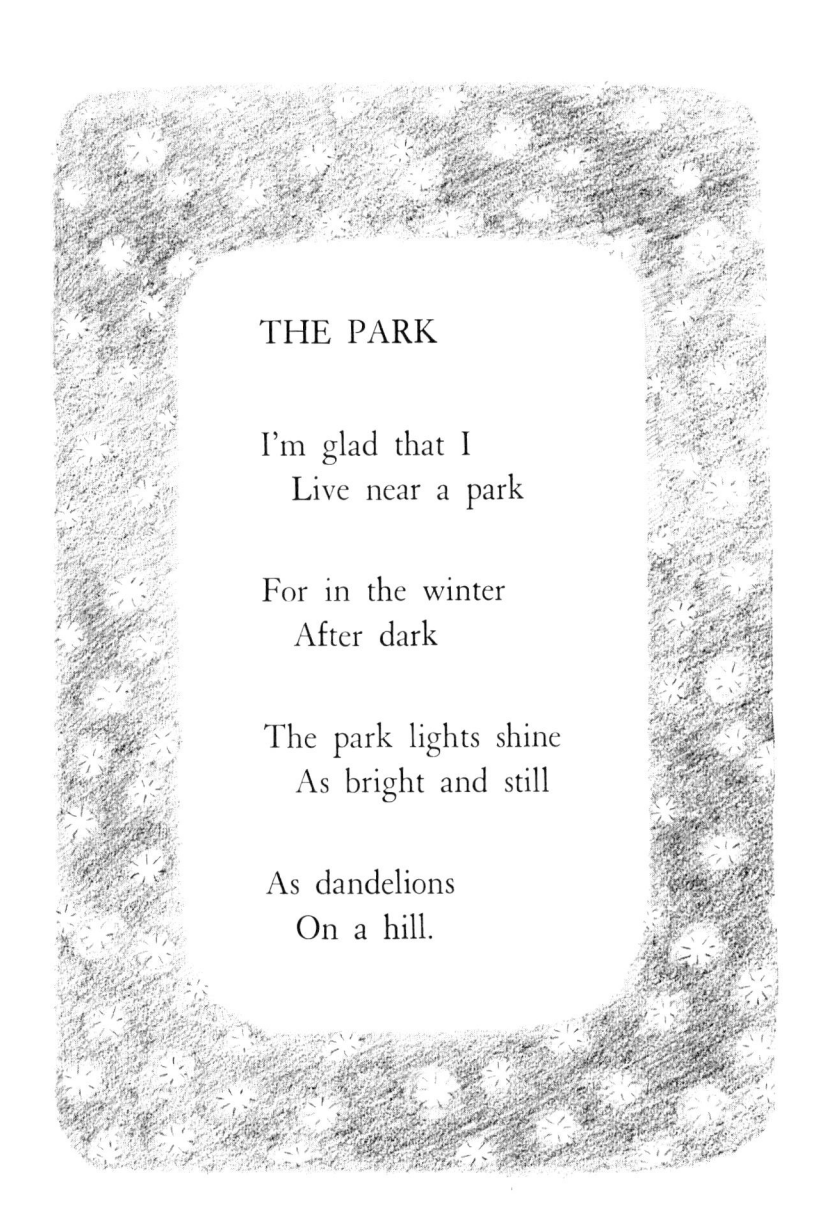

I'm glad that I
  Live near a park

For in the winter
  After dark

The park lights shine
  As bright and still

As dandelions
  On a hill.

PARK PLAY

Every morning
I can play
In the park
Across the way.

I can run
And I can shout.
I am glad
When I come out.

PART TWO
. . . I love to go traveling . . .

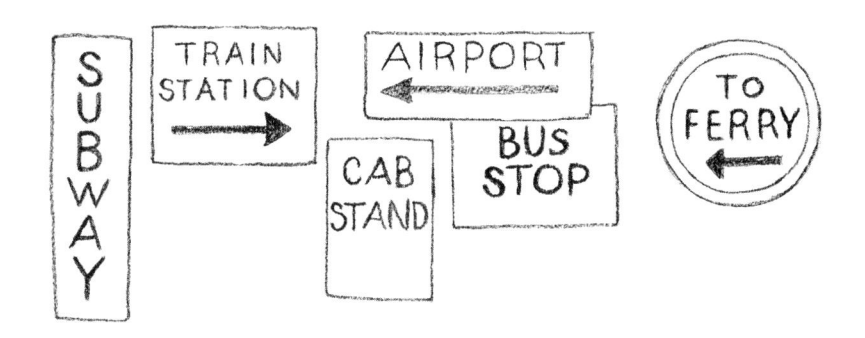

TRAVELING

I go a-traveling,
Traveling, traveling, traveling.
In taxi, in train
I'm off once again.
Oh, I love to go
Traveling, traveling.

Where shall I go a-traveling,
Traveling, traveling, traveling?
On the sea, in the air,
On the land—I don't care,
For I love to go
Traveling, traveling.

UNDERGROUND RUMBLING

At times when we're walking
Along the street
There comes a shivering
Under our feet.

And a hollow, roaring,
Rumbling sound
Seems to come tumbling
Out of the ground.

We've heard it again
And again and again
So of course we know
It's the subway train.

TAXICABS

Taxicabs of yellow,
Taxicabs of red.
See that funny fellow
With scarlet on his head.

Taxicabs of black and white,
Taxicabs of green.
Blue ones left and brown ones right
With orange ones between.

Colors of the rainbow,
Birds of every feather,
Shining as they stop or go,
Flocking all together.

TRUCKS

Big trucks for steel beams,
Big trucks for coal,
Rumbling down the broad streets,
Heavily they roll.

Little trucks for groceries,
Little trucks for bread,
Turning into every street,
Rushing on ahead.

Big trucks, little trucks,
In never ending lines,
Rumble on and rush ahead
While I read their signs.

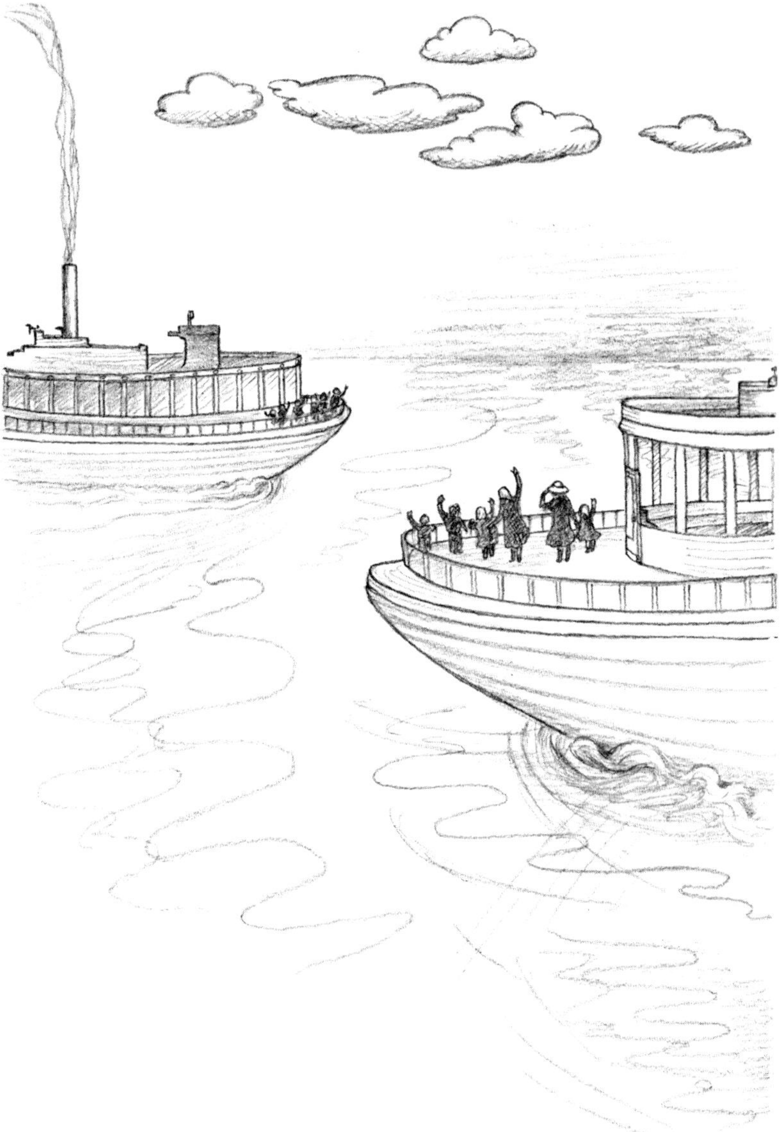

FERRY-BOATS

Over the river,
Over the bay,
Ferry-boats travel
Every day.

Most of the people
Crowd to the side
Just to enjoy
Their ferry-boat ride.

Watching the seagulls,
Laughing with friends,
I'm always sorry
When the ride ends.

TRAINS

Over the mountains,
Over the plains,
Over the rivers,
Here come the trains.

Carrying passengers,
Carrying mail,
Bringing their precious loads
In without fail.

Thousands of freight cars
All rushing on
Through day and darkness,
Through dusk and dawn.

Over the mountains,
Over the plains,
Over the rivers,
Here come the trains.

UP IN THE AIR

Zooming across the sky,
Like a great bird you fly,
    Airplane,
    Silvery white
    In the light.

Turning and twisting in air,
When shall I ever be there,
    Airplane,
    Piloting you
    Far in the blue?

PART THREE
Old Dog lay in the summer sun . . .

BAGGAGE

Don't forget the swimming suits;
Don't forget the thermos;
Don't forget the flashlight
And a lantern for the tent.

Don't forget the blankets;
Don't forget the sweaters;
"Don't forget" was all we heard
For days before we went.

Don't forget the lunch box!
Don't forget the Kodak!
Don't forget the camp stool
And don't forget the books!

"Don't forget! Don't forget!"
But when we came away
We did forget to bring with us
My father's fishing hooks.

MOUNTAIN VIEWS

Up to the top of the mountain!
Up till we touch the sky
Where trees are small and rocks are bare
And clouds go drifting by.

Up to the top of the mountain
Where we stop to see the view
Which stretches away for thirty miles
And the ridges are long and blue.

Up to the top of the mountain
Where we stop awhile and rest
And climb a tower and look away
North, south, and east, and west.

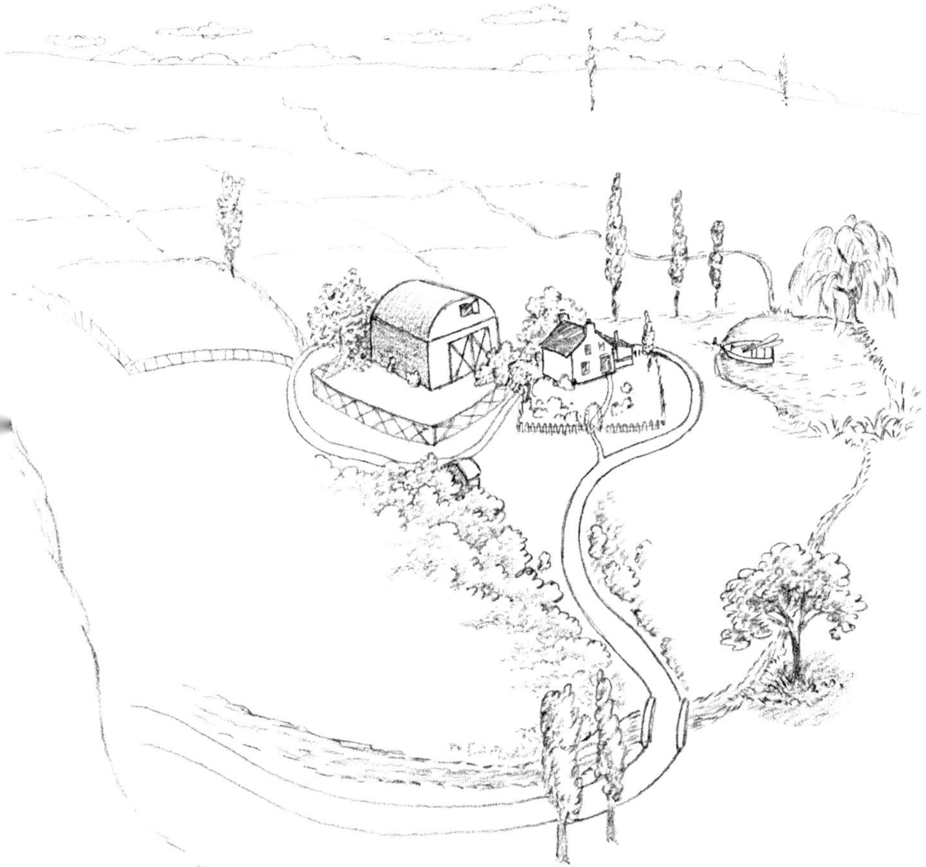

FAMILIAR FRIENDS

The horses, the pigs,
And the chickens,
The turkeys, the ducks
And the sheep!
I can see all my friends
From my window
As soon as I waken
From sleep.

The cat on the fence
Is out walking.
The geese have gone down
For a swim.
The pony comes trotting
Right up to the gate;
He knows I have candy
For him.

The cows in the pasture
Are switching
Their tails to keep off
The flies.
And the old mother dog
Has come out in the yard
With five pups to give me
A surprise.

OVERALLS

See my blue overalls
Trimmed with red
And buttons sewn on
With stout black thread.

I've three roomy pockets
For nails and string,
For hammers or pencils
Or anything.

I'm a good workman
With overalls on;
I'll water the grass
Or cut the lawn.

I'll be a machinist;
I'll grease the car.
I'll be a road-mender
And spread the tar.

I'm dressed in overalls,
So I don't mind.
I'm ready for any job
I can find.

HOUSE FOR BLUEBIRDS

Bluebirds,
Come to this house
Which we have hung
For you and your young.

We made a little porch
Where you can sit.
Please, bluebirds,
Come and look at it.

I will be quiet as a mouse,
If you will build
Your nest in this house,
And lay your eggs,
And hatch your brood.
Our garden will supply
Your food.

Please, bluebirds,
Come to this house
Which we have made.
Don't be afraid.

WADING

This morning I went wading
In the clear pebbly brook.
A school of shiny fishes
Came around my toes to look.

I stood as still
As still can be
To see what they
Would do to me.

Well I guess
Everybody knows
What I did
When they nipped my toes.

GREEN FROG

Bright-eyed, green frog,
Colored like the grass;
Green, sheen-shining frog,
Leap when I pass.

Finish with your croaking,
Chunk-chunk, kerchunk!
Plunge into the water,
Plunk-plunk, kerplunk!

Swim below the water
To a sunken log;
Hide yourself, hide yourself,
Long-legged frog.

TURTLE

I have not heard a turtle talk,
Or even make a sound;
But I have watched a turtle walk—
    Trick-track,
    Trick-track—
Slowly on the ground.

I have not felt a turtle bite,
Or seen it snap its jaws;
But I have followed trick-track trails
Of a turtle's claws.

And I have seen a turtle pull
Its head and legs, and tail as well,
Quickly into safety
Inside its hard clean shell.

CRICKET

Black shiny
Crickety cricket,
Hop quick
Quickety quicket.

My cat is ready
To springety spring.
Jump quick,
Crickety cricketing thing.

Leap to a small crooked
Crackety crack.
Squeezy squeeze in,
And don't scroodge back.

GRASSHOPPER

If I were a grasshopper,
I know what I would do:
I'd move my strong jaws
And chew, chew, chew.

I'd keep my big eyes open
And see, see, see.
I'd stretch my long feelers
All around me.

Then I'd spread my wings
And fly, fly, fly;
And hop, hop away
If a child came by.

WOOLLY BEAR CATERPILLAR

Woolly bear caterpillar
Makes a dusty track.
He's hunting for a winter home;
He humps his fuzzy back.

He seeks a snug and secret place,
For winter's coming soon.
And there in spring he'll stir himself
To weave a strong cocoon.

Then one warm day this woolly bear,
Which now curls in my hand,
Will turn into a tiger moth.
—It's hard to understand.

RED HEN

She turned her head to this side,
   She turned her head to that,
Looking round for tidbits,
   Juicy ones and fat.

Scritchy-scratch went Red Hen's feet,
   Nib-nab went her bill.
She ate of juicy tidbits
   Until she ate her fill.

And then she flew into a nest
   And laid an egg, and then,
With a cut-cut-cut, ca-dah-cut,
   Flew off to eat again.

SMALL RED ANTS

"Who likes bread and sugar?"
"We do," small red ants say.
"Please, won't you drop some tasty crumbs
For us to take away?"

I crumbled bread and sugar.
At once a moving line
Of small red ants went carrying
Those sugared crumbs of mine.

Each grasped a crumb in strong jaws;
On six legs crossed the floor.
And soon the spot where crumbs had dropped
Was cleaner than before.

KITTEN

My gray kitten
Is clean because
She washed her fur
And all her paws.

And I know the words
Of the song she sung
After she washed
With her pink tongue.

Purr-purr, purr-purr,
Purr-purr, purr!
    Purr-purr, purr-purr,
    Purr-purr, purr!

MOTHER'S BOUQUETS

Every day
I gather flowers
And take them to my mother.

Every day
She makes bouquets,
Each prettier than the other.

COMPANY

When I go to my garden,
My little dog goes too.
He wags his tail
And sniffs around,
But I have work to do.

I'm glad he came, for while I work
He keeps me company.
He goes exploring here
And there,
Or sits and watches me.

SUNNING

Old Dog lay in the summer sun
Much too lazy to rise and run.
He flapped an ear
At a buzzing fly.
He winked a half opened
Sleepy eye.
He scratched himself
On an itching spot,
As he dozed on the porch
Where the sun was hot.
He whimpered a bit
From force of habit
While he lazily dreamed
Of chasing a rabbit.
But Old Dog happily lay in the sun
Much too lazy to rise and run.

MY LITTLE RABBIT

I had a little rabbit;
His eyes were shiny bright;
His fur was soft as velvet;
His fluffy tail was white.
But oh! my little rabbit
Died last night.

Now I have put him in a box—
I found one small and trim;
I find it hard to dig his grave
Because my eyes are dim;
But oh! my rabbit died last night
And I must bury him.

DUCKS IN THE RAIN

Ducks are dabbling in the rain,
Dibbling, dabbling in the rain.
Drops of water from each back
Scatter as ducks flap and quack.

I can only stand and look
From my window at the brook,
For I cannot flap and quack
And scatter raindrops from my back.

PART FOUR
. . . tracks in the snow.

WHICH?

When I am in the country
I like the trees and grass.
I like the cows and horses,
I count them as I pass.

When I am in the city
I like the city streets.
I like the trucks and taxis
Passing by in fleets.

"The city or the country?"
I sometimes say to Mother,
"I cannot say which one I like
Better than the other."

AUTUMN WOODS

I like the woods
   In autumn
When dry leaves hide the ground,
When the trees are bare
And the wind sweeps by
With a lonesome rushing sound.

I can rustle the leaves
   In autumn
And I can make a bed
In the thick dry leaves
That have fallen
From the bare trees
Overhead.

BIRDS AT TWILIGHT

In the late afternoon
When the long shadows fall
And the sun disappears in the west,
The pigeons and sparrows,
The robins and jays
Get ready for sleep and for rest.

They sing and they murmur;
They hop on the ground;
Each preens himself with his bill.
Then they fly to a bush
Or a sheltering tree
And tuck down their heads and sit still.

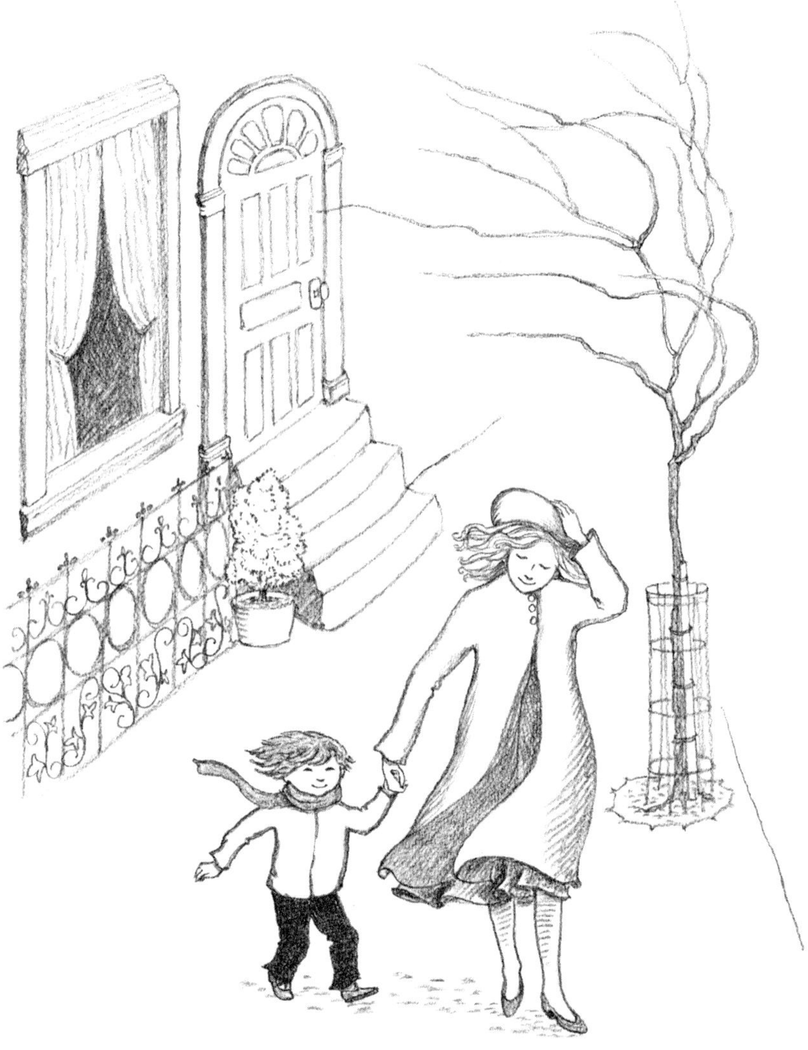

WINDY ∮ WEATHER

"Ugh!" cried Windy Weather,
  "I'm as wild as I can be.
I break-shake the shutter;
  I smash-lash the tree.

"I whip-zip the dust along;
  I whang-bang the door;
I blow-throw the hats away;
  I mop-flop the floor.

"I bowl-roll the storm clouds
  Across gray angry skies.
Look out! Beware! I might catch you
  Quickly by surprise."

PLAY AFTER RAIN

The rain has stopped
And Mother says I may
Put on all my rubber things
And hurry out to play.

So I pull on my rubber boots,
My rubber coat and hat,
And go where muddy puddles
Are lying smooth and flat.

When Billy comes along
We soon think up a game.
"Stepping in the Muddy Puddles"
Is its name.

We step in every puddle
Oh, most, *most* carefully.
Sometimes I follow Billy;
Sometimes he follows me.

Although we wore our rubber things
We got quite soaking wet,
And Mother says we made a game
She hopes we will forget.

TRACKS IN THE SNOW

I follow tracks
In the white, new snow,
Looking and looking
To find where they go.

Off over there
Runs a small bird's track;
Three toes in front
And one in back.

My big dog's tracks
Show deep and strong
Where his bare pads
Went trotting along.

My white cat's tracks
Are cautious and neat;
She doesn't like snow
On her soft feet.

But everywhere, anywhere
My tracks go,
Following other tracks
In the snow.

THE ICICLE

An icicle, hanging from our roof,
Said to the sun this morning,
"I'll freeze your finger
If you touch me.
I'm giving you fair warning."

The sun didn't answer a single word,
But he wrinkled his face in a smile
And became so warm
That I could not see
Any icicle after a while.

SNOWMAN

"Our snowman won't be cold at all,"
   Billy said to Sue,
"Although he has to stand outside
   The winter night through.

"His hands and ears are covered,
   And anyone can tell
That his hat fits snugly on his head
   And his suit is buttoned well."

A CITY STREET AT CHRISTMAS

All along
The city street
Busy Christmas shoppers
Meet.

I like walking there
Because
I can talk
With Santa Claus,

And at windows
Make long stops,
Or gaze into
The candy shops.

We walk along
On many nights
To see the show
Of Christmas lights.

COUNTING THE DAYS

How many days to Christmas?
Forty, thirty, and then . . .
Twenty-five, twenty, seventeen,
Fourteen, eleven, ten.

Nine eight seven—six five four—
Three days, two days, slowly go.
But the last day before Christmas
Is slow . . . slow . . . slow.

MATILDA JANE AND I

My doll has a red dress.
She has curly hair.
She sits before the fireplace
In a little old chair.

I sit close beside her
In a little old chair too.
She has a smile upon her face
And her eyes are blue.

We watch the flames rush upward
And the sparks fly,
While we wait for Mother,
Matilda Jane and I.

WRAPPING PRESENTS

Paper! Ribbon!
Stickers! String!
We can wrap
Most anything.

Mother says
She thinks I'm quick
At learning how
To cut and stick.

But ribbon bows
I cannot tie,
Although I try
And try and try.

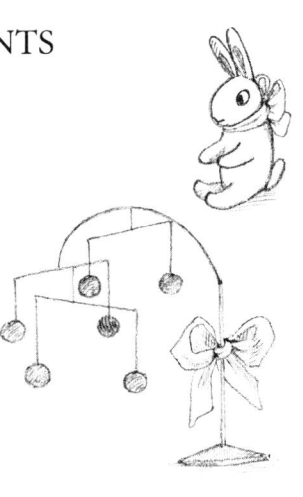

MY CHRISTMAS TREE

Shine, Christmas Tree, shine!
Shine, shine, shine!
You are mine.
With your tinselly strands
And your shimmering bands;
With your glittering star,
You are mine, Christmas Tree,
You are.

Shine, Christmas Tree, shine!
Shine, shine, shine!
You are mine.
With your snowy popcorn,
Colored balls, silver horn;
With your lights all aglow,
You are mine, Christmas Tree,
I know.

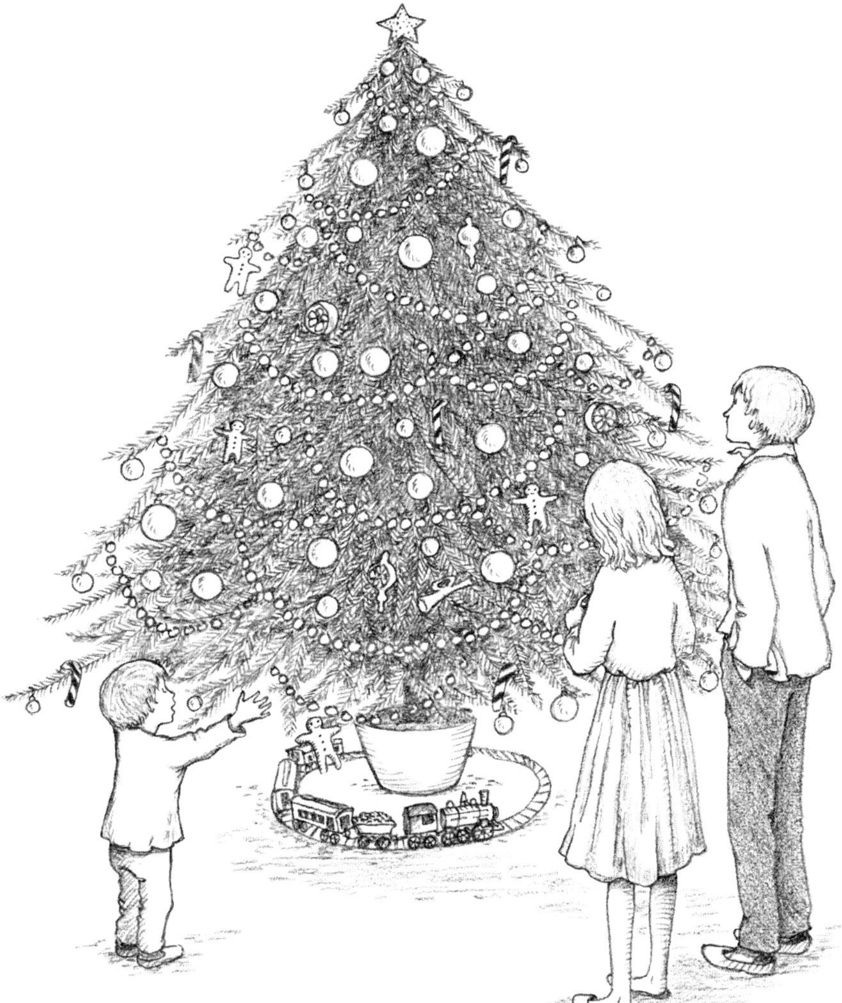

THE YEAR MOVES ON

The snow has melted;
The ice has gone;
Spring rain is falling,
The year moves on.

Spring rain is washing
Everything clean
And bringing fresh clothes
Of new soft green.

Birds are peeping
With heads half out
From holes and places
Round about.

Across the fields
The sun shines through
And it's come-come-coming
To shine on you.

List of Titles

    APARTMENT HOUSES   4
    AUTUMN WOODS   60
    BAGGAGE   33
    BIRDS AT TWILIGHT   61
    BUILDING A SKYSCRAPER   14
    A CITY STREET AT CHRISTMAS   70
    COMPANY   52
    COUNTING THE DAYS   71
    CRICKET   45
    DUCKS IN THE RAIN   56
    FAMILIAR FRIENDS   36
    FERRY-BOATS   27
    FOURTH FLOOR!   7
    GRASSHOPPER   46
    GREEN FROG   43
    GROCERIES   6

HOUSE FOR BLUEBIRDS   40
THE ICICLE   68
IN THE CITY   3
KITTEN   50
MATILDA JANE AND I   72
MOTHER'S BOUQUETS   51
MOUNTAIN VIEWS   34
MY CHRISTMAS TREE   74
MY LITTLE RABBIT   54
OVERALLS   38
THE PARK   17
PARK PLAY   18
PEOPLE   16
PLAY AFTER RAIN   64
RED HEN   48
THE ROOF   12
"SH!"   10
SMALL RED ANTS   49
SNOWMAN   69
SOMETIMES   8
SUNNING   53
TAXICABS   23
TRACKS IN THE SNOW   66
TRAINS   28
TRAVELING   21

TRUCKS   24
TURTLE   44
UNDERGROUND RUMBLING   22
UP IN THE AIR   30
WADING   42
WHICH?   59
WINDY WEATHER   63
WITH MY BUILDING SET   11
WOOLLY BEAR CATERPILLAR   47
WRAPPING PRESENTS   73
THE YEAR MOVES ON   76

JAMES S. TIPPETT (1885–1958) was born in Memphis, Missouri. He received a B.S. degree from the University of Missouri and taught in schools all over the country until 1954, when he retired to concentrate entirely on writing for young children. During his lifetime, Mr. Tippett wrote more than twenty-five books, and his stories and poems continue to be anthologized.

About his poetry, James Tippett said: "Almost always I write about something I have seen or done as a child, or have found out that other children like to see and do. I remember many things that were important to my childhood life, and these are things young readers will find in my writing."

MARY CHALMERS was born in Camden, New Jersey, and studied art at the Philadelphia Museum School and the Barnes Foundation. She is the author-artist of THROW A KISS, HARRY; TAKE A NAP, HARRY; and BE GOOD, HARRY, as well as A CHRISTMAS STORY and other popular books for children. Ms. Chalmers lives in Haddon Heights, New Jersey. She has many cats and is active in the Animal Welfare Association of Camden.

Format by Anne E. Brown
Set in 14 pt Granjon
Composed by American Book–Stratford Press
Printed by Halliday Lithograph Corporation
Bound by American Book–Stratford Press
HARPER & ROW, PUBLISHERS, INC.

DATE DUE

MAR 2 9 1983	FEB 1 9 1991		
APR 1 0 1983	DEC 1 7 1991		
MAR 2 3 RECD	OCT 04 1992		
APR 0 8 1984	FEB 1 1 1999		
MAR 2 1 RECD	MAR 0 4 1999		
OCT 2 3 1984	APR 3 0 1999		
OCT 0 4 RECD	APR 1 7 2003		
OCT 2 1986	APR 1 4 2003		
SEP FEB 2 0 1991			
DEC 1 7 1991			
APR 0 9 1992			
MAR 3 0 1992			
APR 1 7 2008			
			Printed in USA
	261-2500		